Social Impact Investing
New Agenda In Fighting Poverty

Kim Tan and Brian Griffiths

Transformational Business Network
London

First published in 2016 in Great Britain by
Transformational Business Network
Fifth Floor, 11 Leadenhall Street
London EC3V 1LP

and

Anchor Recordings Ltd
DPTT, Synegis House, 21 Crockhamwell Road,
Woodley, Reading RG5 3LE

For further information, contact:
Transformational Business Network
Fifth Floor,
11 Leadenhall Street
London EC3V 1LP

ISBN 978-1-911173-09-0

Printed by Lightning Source

Contents

Preface to second monograph

Much has changed in the field of social impact investing since we wrote the first monograph on 'Fighting poverty through enterprise' in 2008.

The sector has now expanded significantly. The case for social venture capital is well established and widely accepted, and many leading institutions in the fight against poverty are now investing in it substantially. Two reports describing this expansion are worthy of mention: JPMorgan (2010) *Impact investments – an emerging asset class*, and The World Economic Forum (September 2013) *From the margins to mainstream*. At the same time, a number of social impact businesses are pursuing a public listing of their shares to allow retail investors access to this new asset class. This new monograph includes a chapter describing the social impact investment universe.

This expansion has led to a proliferation of both terminology and investment funds. Many are increasingly using the term 'impact investing' to describe it, as proposed by the Rockefeller Foundation in 2008. The proliferation of terms and practices in this area has not been without controversy, a subject that Chapter 4 addresses.

These developments have occurred against a backdrop of continued significant progress in the fight against poverty, although this progress remains patchy. Not all the Millennium

Development Goals (MDGs) were met by the 2015 deadline, but substantial numbers of people have been lifted out of extreme poverty, many more children (and especially girls) are in school, and diseases such as malaria and measles are in retreat. This new monograph contains updated data on these issues.

Finally, we have expanded and brought up to date the case studies of specific impact investments. These investee companies have scaled up and expanded significantly and are impressive examples of social venture investing.

We wish to thank Emma Pedrick for her excellent research and editorial work, without which this monograph would not have been possible.

Kim Tan and Brian Griffiths

(February 2016)

Introduction

Despite common misconceptions, huge progress has been made in the fight against poverty over recent years, as described in the next chapter. Furthermore, it is widely accepted that this progress owes more to enterprise and economic growth than it does to international aid.[1]

Therefore, the urgent question we must now address is: How can we further encourage and upscale private enterprise in poor countries?

This is a question that the business community is well placed to answer. Indeed, we believe that there is a moral imperative for the business community to engage. Their involvement could make a huge difference to the millions of people who still experience the daily grind of material poverty. This monograph explains both why and how they should engage, and gives examples of real-world investment in poor countries.

---

1. For a quick summary, see 'Towards the end of poverty,' The Economist, published 01/06/13, accessed 29/02/16: http://www.economist.com/ news/ leaders/21578665-nearly-1-billion-people-have-been-taken-out- extreme-poverty-20-years-world-should-aim

1 Grounds for hope

Over the 20 years up to 2008, the proportion of the global population living in extreme poverty halved. The speed of progress actually increased over this period, with people lifting themselves out of poverty at a faster rate than ever before. More than two billion people have gained access to clean drinking water. At the same time, the number of young children who die each day has halved (from 34,000 to 17,000), despite population growth. Diseases such as malaria and measles are in retreat, and more children are in school than ever before.[2]

These improvements are unprecedented in history, and are largely due to private enterprise: more than 90% of jobs in developing countries are created by the private sector (see Chapter 2).[3]

Despite these gains, progress is patchy and incomplete. For example, while the proportion of people living on just $2 a day has fallen, population growth means that the absolute number living on $2 a day actually rose between 1981 and 1996, although it has fallen slightly since then.[4] Furthermore, the UN indicates that in terms of the absolute number of people living in slums, the number has grown from 689 million in 1990 to an estimate of more than 880 million currently.[5] And despite falling slightly over recent years, the number of people who remain undernourished remains about 780 million, or 13% of the world population[6] a scandal in a world where there is so much food waste.

Progress also varies significantly across geographical regions. In 1990, 61% of China's population lived in extreme poverty, compared with 52% in Southern Asia, and 57% in sub-Saharan Africa. By 2015, the comparable figures were 4% in China, 17% in Southern Asia and 41% in sub-Saharan Africa.[7] China's poverty alleviation correlates with its economic growth, with annual rates as high as 10% since 1990.

Progress in all regions is also somewhat precarious. The recession which followed the global financial crisis, and associated food and fuel crises, are likely to have pushed between 60 and 90 million people back into poverty.[8] At the same time, many of those who have recently escaped poverty remain in fragile employment, with no recourse to public safety nets. This risk is felt more acutely by women, who are much more likely than men to be in vulnerable employment.

Environmental pressures – not least the increasingly obvious impacts of climate change – are likely to compound this vulnerability. International development agency Tearfund already reports that its partners on the ground are struggling with the impact of climate change, with reservoirs running dry and rainfall becoming increasingly erratic. More than 1.2 billion people already live in water basins where usage exceeds sustainable limits, and by 2025 more than two-thirds of the global population are likely to be living in water-stressed conditions.[9]

In addition, growing inequality may represent a systemic threat to further poverty reduction. The last few years have seen an increasing focus on inequality trends. Oxfam's recent claim that the richest 1% now own more than the rest of the world combined made headlines around the world.[10] Regardless of the debate around this specific claim, growing inequality may pose a risk for three reasons.

Firstly, access to basic (and increasingly scarce) resources such as water often depends on purchasing power. As those at the top of the income distribution (locally or globally) consume more, those at the bottom can be priced out of the market. Secondly, inequality of income and wealth tends to lead to inequalities of power. All over the world, economic elites are able to tilt the playing field in their favour, facilitating corruption, natural resource grabs and other rent-seeking activities. Thirdly, research by the International Monetary Fund (IMF) suggests that economic growth itself is inhibited by excessive levels of inequality. Inequality can choke the economic engine itself.

Despite these challenges, the sharp reduction in extreme poverty in all low-income regions of the world, including sub-Saharan Africa, is indisputable. And there is a growing global consensus around these issues. The Millennium Development Goals (MDGs), which expired in 2015, have been replaced by the Global Goals (also known as the Sustainable Development Goals). These are a broader set of targets embracing multi-dimensional poverty, social justice and environmental degradation. They were the result of a wide-ranging consultation process involving national governments, civil society and business, and set a new target of eradicating extreme poverty by 2030. (The MDGs aimed to halve extreme poverty by 2015.)

While this target is ambitious, there are reasons for hope. Alongside a growing international consensus, other factors are also playing a positive role. Remittances (the money sent home by migrants) now represents a huge cash injection for many poor countries. In 2014 remittances totalled twice as much as official development aid provided by governments.[11] The importance of this source of support to families and the national economy cannot be underestimated. According to World Bank Chief Economist

Kaushik Basu, *'Israel and India have shown how macro liquidity crises can be managed by tapping into the wealth of diaspora communities. Mexican migrants have boosted the construction sector. Tajikistan manages to nearly double its consumption by using remittance money. Migrants and remittances are clearly major players in today's global economy.'*[12]

And the increase in South–South cooperation (ie cooperation between non-developed countries) is also encouraging. While much of the media has focused on the role of China, investment from and collaboration between other emerging and developing countries is also increasing. These investments are not without controversy (with some land acquisition – or 'land grabs' – displacing local farmers without remuneration, for example). Many, however, are positive and, at the very least, investments in Africa demonstrate that the region which The Economist famously labelled as the 'hopeless continent' a decade ago is more attractive to foreign investment. In this regard it is worth noting that, according to the World Bank's 'ease of doing business' ratings, Rwanda now ranks just behind Luxembourg and Greece, with Botswana and South Africa not far behind.[13]

Yet, even greater gains in poverty reduction will be necessary if we are to empower all those currently mired in extreme poverty to live lives free of malnutrition, disease and corruption. Furthermore, continued economic divergence between the poorest regions and the rest of the world is likely to fuel illegal migration, terrorism and conflict. In the long run, these threats can only be addressed through development. The following chapters will consider how best to do this.

Notes to Chapter 1

2. Stats sourced from the World Bank, United Nations and European Commission, as quoted in Evans and Gower (2015) The restorative economy, Tearfund, with the exception of the drinking water statistic, available at: http://www.un.org/millenniumgoals/environ.shtml
3. See http://www.ifc.org/wps/wcmconnect/0fe6e2804e2c0a8f8d3bad7a9dd66321/IFC_FULL+JOB+STUDY+REPORT_JAN2013_FINAL.pdf?MOD=AJPERES
4. See http://www.un.org/esa/socdev/rwss/docs/2010/chapter2.pdf
5. http://www.un.org/millenniumgoals/2015_MDG_Report/pdf/MDG%20 2015%20rev%20(July%201).pdf
6. Ibid
7. Ibid
8. McCord and Vandermoortele (2009) The global financial crisis: poverty and social protection, Overseas Development Institute Briefing Paper, available at: http://www.odi.org/sites/odi.org.uk/files/odi-assets/publications-opinion-files/4285.pdf
9. Evans and Gower (2015) The restorative economy, Tearfund
10. http://www.bloomberg.com/news/articles/2016-01-18/richest-1-now-wealthier-than-the-rest-of-the-world-oxfam-says
11. World Bank (2015) Migration and Development Brief 24, available at: https://siteresources.worldbank.org/INTPROSPECTS/Resources/334934-1288990760745/MigrationandDevelopmentBrief24.pdf
12. World Bank press release, issued 13/04/15, accessed 29/02/16, available at: http://www.worldbank.org/en/news/press-release/2015/04/13/remittances-growth-to-slow-sharply-in-2015-as-europe-and-russia-stay-weak-pick-up-expected-next-year
13. 'Economy Rankings' for June 2012, published by Doing Business, International Finance Corporation. Published 20 June 2013 and available here: http://www.doingbusiness.org/rankings

2 Why aid will never be enough . . .

For the past five decades, the main approach that governments have taken to tackle global poverty has been government-to-government aid. Foreign aid as we have known it over recent decades started with President Truman's Point Four Program, as outlined in his inaugural address of January 1949: *'We must embark on a bold new programme for... the improvement and growth of underdeveloped areas. More than half the people of the world are living in conditions approaching misery... For the first time in history, humanity possesses the knowledge and the skill to relieve the suffering of the people.'*

Between then and 2008, US $2.3 trillion was given in aid, according to estimates by William Easterly, professor at New York University and a former World Bank economist. Richard Dowden, director of the Royal African Society, estimates that, over a similar period, Africa has received about US $1 trillion, which equates to roughly US $5,000 for every African living today if it were distributed evenly at today's prices.[14]

Some have argued that, because of the success of the Marshall Plan extended by the US to help Europe recover from the Second World War, there should be the equivalent of a Marshall Plan for Africa today. However, Dowden estimates that, over the past 50 years, aid to Africa has been roughly the equivalent of six Marshall Plans. The reality is that the plight of Europe in 1945 and that of Africa today are very different.

Frequently, donor governments and aid agencies demonstrate their commitment to tackling global poverty by the volume of aid they provide. But this is to confuse what we could call 'inputs' and 'outputs.' Aid is an 'input' to development: 'outputs' are poverty reduction, provision of schooling, improvements in health, and so on. The major reason aid has been subject to so much criticism is not because of a shortfall in volume (input) but because of its ineffectiveness in terms of output.

Recently, a number of prominent voices have criticised the effectiveness of aid. Experts, such as Angus Deaton (Princeton professor and Nobel Prize winner), have argued that aid can actually inhibit development. Others, including Paul Collier (professor at Oxford), have suggested that poverty traps such as chronic conflict, poor governance systems or being 'landlocked with bad neighbours' render aid ineffective. Others, such as Mohammad Yunus (Grameen Bank) and Professor William Easterly (New York University), have argued for a radically different approach to aid spending.

Three criticisms stand out in particular.
Firstly, it is claimed that aid can encourage inefficiency and waste. Easterly argues that aid is often ineffective because donors have little incentive to make aid work well ('Who loses their job if the project in question doesn't work?'). As The Journal of Economic Affairs noted in December 2003, *'National and international aid bureaucracies, in alliance with assorted consultants, academics and NGOs, have a vested interest in the aid business, mostly with little regard to policy results.'*

The World Bank has estimated that 60% of all foreign aid stays within donor countries and is used to pay for consultants, to purchase nationally produced goods and for transportation costs. The late Indian prime minister, Rajiv Gandhi, conjectured that less than 15 cents in each dollar of aid actually reaches poor beneficiaries. The charitable, NGO and philanthropic sector in the USA alone is an annual US $240 billion industry. This is a huge 'third sector' with vested interests in the aid business and with money and institutional interests at stake.

Second is the charge that aid can distort local economies. Poor countries often do not have the capacity to absorb a huge inflow of aid dollars, and the resulting appreciation of local currency in foreign exchange markets can make exports less competitive. This can harm the very people aid is intended to help. Similarly, when aid is delivered in the form of goods from donor countries, from food to shelters, this can put local suppliers out of business, by reducing the price of these goods in local markets.

Third, aid can be an incentive for developing country governments to pursue perverse political agendas because foreign aid is government to government. Clearly, the requirements attached to aid are typically intended to help those in poverty. However, Easterly concludes that over the past 40 years those countries that have developed successfully have neither received much in foreign aid nor followed the prescriptions given by Western institutions. In fact, worst of all, aid can foster corruption, with all the negative consequences this brings.

Finally, and related to this, it has proved difficult in economic research to find any reliable relationship between aid and economic growth. In their influential paper published in 2000, World Bank economists Burnside and Dollar showed that *'aid has a positive impact on growth in developing countries with good fiscal, monetary and trade policies, but has little effect in the presence of poor policies.'* Their first conclusion, that aid has a positive impact in countries with good policies (low budget deficits, low inflation, free trade), suggested that aid should not be given across the board but focused on those countries with good policies. It was on this basis that the US set up the Millennium Challenge Corporation with extra funding and developed 16 indicators of what constituted good policies.

However, using new data for a longer time period and more data from the original period, Easterly, Levine and Roodman found that there was no evidence that aid even increased growth in countries with good policies.

On the contrary, there is evidence that aid has a negative impact on the GDP of recipient countries as shown by the graph below. Whilst aid to Africa increased from 5% to 17% of GDP in the late 1990s, GDP growth actually decreased from 2% to zero or negative growth. The worrying conclusion: There is no demonstrable direct relationship between aid and poverty reduction.

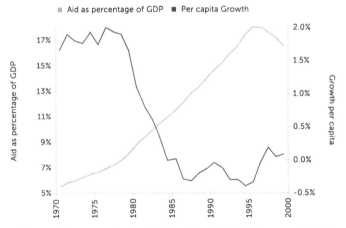

Aid and Growth in Africa
(10 year moving averages)

Source: European Centre for International Political Economy Analysis of World Development Indicators, 30 June, 2008.

Their second conclusion, after 50 years of aid, is surely self-evident: historical evidence suggests that good governance and policies help economies grow and reduce poverty, whether countries receive aid or not. The late Peter Bauer devoted most of his academic life to exposing the flaws and failures of foreign aid, having lived in Malaya (now Malaysia) and studied its rubber industry, as well as the problems of primary producers and trade in West Africa. In 1998 to mark the 50th anniversary of the inception of foreign aid, he wrote (with Cranley Onslow) an essay entitled Fifty years of failure. His conclusion was that foreign aid had not only not helped, but had positively harmed the poor in developing countries. It encouraged inefficiency and waste, he contested, and the adoption of perverse policies by developing country governments. His recommendation was simple: government-to-government handouts should be ended.

Is there any good aid?
Clearly, there is a real and substantial danger of aid actually harming those that it is intended to help. Unfortunately, there are numerous examples of this in the literature. However, this does not preclude the possibility of 'good aid.' Indeed, when spent well, aid can support the agenda we set out in this paper: supporting private enterprise. In fact, there are a number of clear examples of this.[15]

Businesses need roads and other infrastructure, and areas such as healthcare and education are clearly best addressed with the involvement of governments and NGOs, for example. Two recent innovations in the field of healthcare offer compelling illustrations of good aid.

Gavi, the global vaccines alliance, was created in 2000 to improve access to new (and old, under-used) vaccines for children in poor countries. It was initially financed by the issuance of 'vaccine bonds' in the capital markets, backed financially by long-term pledges from aid donor governments, and with the support of the Bill and Melinda Gates Foundation. As a public-private partnership, Gavi attempts to bring together the best of the UN, pharmaceutical industry, governments and civil society. By providing advance market commitments (AMCs), Gavi creates a market for vaccine development and, by pooling demand, it also gains market power, helping to keep vaccines affordable. So far, it has helped developing countries immunise 500 million children, preventing about 7 million deaths.

The Global Fund to Fight AIDS, Tuberculosis and Malaria has had similar success, supporting programmes estimated to have averted 17 million deaths since 2002. The Fund's rigorous focus on impact, monitoring and transparency underpins this achievement.

So-called 'aid for trade' can be another key area where foreign government support makes a tangible difference. If developing countries are to grow more rapidly and reduce poverty, they need access to the markets of developed countries. However, despite initiatives such as the EU's Everything But Arms (EBA) agreement, where the poorest countries receive duty-free access to the European market, these countries can face serious infrastructural and institutional obstacles to increasing trade. As Trade Matters, a publication of the UK government overseas development agency DFID, comments: *'Supporting the continued reduction in trade barriers worldwide will not help developing countries greatly unless there is a simultaneous commitment to improve the capacity of those countries to take advantage of new trading opportunities which arise.'* Of course, social venture capital has a key role to play here, but aid for trade focused on institutional reform and key elements of infrastructure can also play a role. In their review of the evidence in this field, the World Trade Organisation and OECD estimate that for every $1 of aid for trade, exports typically increase by $8.[16]

Another recent example is the cancellation of the foreign debt of poor countries. As a result of the Jubilee 2000 campaign, the G8 countries together with the IMF and World Bank launched the Highly Indebted Poor Countries (HIPC) debt restructuring initiative. This led to the cancellation of more than US $60 billion of debt from 26 countries. Since 2006, the Multilateral Debt Relief Initiative (MDRI) has continued debt relief to poor countries, and together these programmes have helped '36 countries, 30 of them in Africa, providing $75 billion in debt-service relief.' [17]

Debt cancellation has had its critics. The main issue is whether the cancellation of debts will lead to further irresponsible behaviour by political leaders in Highly Indebted Poor Countries. Will the money saved from interest payments be used wisely by these leaders in the interests of their people? These are valid concerns and yet a number of points need to be made in its defence.

First, debt restructuring occurs every day between banks and corporations. In many instances, and as part of the restructuring, there is an element of debt cancellation. Bad debts that are irrecoverable have to be cancelled in order that companies are able to restructure. Is there any difference between this and bad debts owed by sovereign states?

Second, debt cancellation can have conditionalities imposed on the debtor nation that significantly benefit the poor. In Tanzania and Burundi, money saved as a result of their debt relief programmes has been used successfully to provide universal free primary school education.

Third, although debt cancellation is not a legal right of poor countries, it is a moral responsibility for donor countries. Crippling levels of debt interest can prevent poor countries from providing education, health and shelter, for example.

The need for private enterprise

However, aid itself will never be enough for poor countries and their citizens to escape poverty. As we noted earlier, 90% of jobs in poor countries are created by the private sector, and so ultimately private enterprise is the key to progress in this regard. The four Asian Tigers – Hong Kong, South Korea, Singapore and Taiwan –transformed their economies by supporting enterprise and foreign direct investment, not through aid or philanthropy. In recent years, China and India have similarly begun reforming their economies and millions of their citizens have lifted themselves out of poverty through enterprise.

At a local level, the same is true: situating a factory in an area of high unemployment can transform the region more effectively than providing humanitarian aid. Intentionally building a new factory close to a slum, creating jobs and contributing to the local economy through its monthly wage bill, can be far more effective in tackling poverty than a grant-based Corporate Social Responsibility (CSR) programme.

The large aid agencies and their governments are increasingly recognising the importance of enterprise. As the UK government's White Paper on Eliminating World Poverty noted, *'It is the private sector – from farmers and street* *traders to foreign investors – that creates growth. Growth is fuelled by the creativity and hard work of entrepreneurs and workers.'*

The huge expansion of microcredit in recent years also reflects this change in emphasis. Micro-finance institutions (MFIs) provide small un-collateralised loans ('microcredit' of a few hundred dollars or less) to poor entrepreneurs so they can start up micro-businesses. The loan repayment rate among MFIs is exceptionally high (usually greater than 90%), especially if loans are made to women rather than men.

Since its humble beginnings in 1971, when Opportunity International, a Christian not-for-profit organisation, began lending in Colombia, followed by Accion International in 1973, microfinance has grown to become a multi- billion-dollar industry. In 2004, the International Finance Corporation (IFC, a subsidiary of the World Bank) had outstanding loans to micro- or small/medium-sized enterprises of approximately $25 billion through its partners. By 2014, this had risen to more than $250 billion.[18]

The Grameen Bank, which started in 1976, has become the poster child for micro-credit, with its model of offering very small loans to groups of women. To qualify, Grameen's female customers have to earn less than a dollar a day. Group members are required to monitor each other at weekly meetings, where social pressure helps to ensure repayment. As loans are repaid, people are allowed to borrow more. The group in effect replaces the security that pawnshops gain from collateral. Such is Grameen's success that mainstream banking groups such as Citigroup and India's ICICI have joined the market.

Micro-credit is not a magic bullet for poverty reduction, but it can make a big difference, especially to those in the most extreme poverty. The poor are often credit constrained, in the sense that they cannot access the finance required to turn good business ideas into real businesses, or to acquire the skills (or medical care) to allow them to work. Micro-credit overcomes these hurdles.

However, according to Dr Vinay Samuel of The Bridge Foundation (India), it is estimated that only 3–5% of people with microcredit go on to establish higher levels of income. Other evidence also suggests that many poor people would much rather have a regular job than the uncertainty of running a micro-enterprise. In developed countries, where there are high levels of access to credit and business support, 90% of the workforce are employees rather than small entrepreneurs. In this regard, Banerjee and Duflo have convincingly demonstrated that micro-entrepreneurship in poor countries is often driven by necessity rather than a desire to own one's own business.[19]

Clearly, what is required is to identify and support those entrepreneurs who can successfully build their microenterprise into a fully fledged business able to employ others. Dr Vinay Samuel estimates that perhaps 10–20% of the recipients of microcredit have the necessary skills to do this. It is this issue to which we turn in the next section.

Notes to Chapter 2

14. http://www.theguardian.com/society/2005/jan/09/
internationalaidanddevelopment.aids

15. (http://www.economist.com/news/finance-and-economics/21612183-new-research-suggests-development-aid-does-foster-growthbut-what-cost-aid)

16. WTO and OECD (2013) 'Evaluating the effectiveness of aid for trade': chapter 5 in Aid for trade at a glance, 2013, World Trade Organisation and OECD

17. IMF (2015) 'Debt relief under the Heavily Indebted Poor Countries Initiative,' IMF Factsheet, available here:
https://www.imf.org/external/ np/exr/facts/hipc.htm

18. http:/wwwifcorgwpswcmconnect/3bbf9f004b4f59388b92fb4149c6fa94/
IFC Factsheets_Global rgb_ONLINE.pdf?MOD=AJPERES

19. Banerjee and Duflo (2011) Poor economics, PublicAffairs

3 New agenda: The case for social impact investing

As we have established, the business community has much to offer to help tackle global poverty. Entrepreneurs can use the same skills and expertise that have enabled them to build successful businesses in developed countries, and apply their talents and resources to the problem of enterprise in poor countries. We call this approach impact investment or social venture investing. These are for-profit investments in small/medium-size enterprises (SMEs) in developing countries. They take an enterprise approach to poverty alleviation by building commercially sustainable companies that create jobs and empower the poor to improve their livelihoods. They adopt the principles, discipline and accountability of venture capital investing but with a sub-venture capital rate of financial returns.

Henry Ford once said: *'A business that only makes money is a poor kind of business'.* Most businesses exist solely to make a profit for their shareholders: that is the financial bottom line. Impact investment does not require the same high rate of financial return because it is also seeking social and environmental returns. In other words, it is not investing purely for a financial return. That is not to say that it loses money. In order for the businesses to be sustainable, they have to be profitable.

SMEs as the key to development

We will now highlight several key issues that are not often discussed in the context of the causes of structural poverty. The backbone of developed country economies is the SME (Small-medium enterprises) sector. This sector creates an average of 65% of jobs in high-income countries, compared with only 30% or less in low-income countries (LICs). The absence of a strong SME sector in developing countries has been called the 'missing middle.'

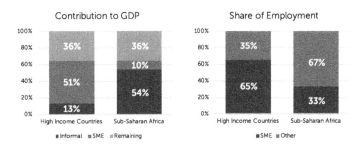

Source: Small and medium enterprise Across the Globe: A new Database, Ayyagari, Beck & Demirguc-kunt, The World Bank Development Research Group, August 2005; 'Venture Capital for Development', Patricof & Sunderland, August 2005. SMEs defined according to each country's official definition of SME, usually up to 250 employees. Africa data set comprised 10 countries whose media SME share of employment was 26.36%.

In addition to creating jobs, SMEs offer a number of other economic benefits:

Sources of entrepreneurship and innovation:
SMEs provide an ideal environment for training in all aspects of business and also a place where new entrepreneurs can be groomed. Seventy-five per cent of all new businesses are started by people who have been previously employed in another company.

Driver of competition:
SMEs drive competition through their greater numbers. Competition in turn will drive innovation, leading to new business start-ups.

Tax-raising potential:
As well as creating jobs, the SME sector also pays tax. Increasing the tax base plays an important role in helping poor countries develop. Sadly, aid, philanthropy and even micro-finance, however well intentioned, can sometimes promote the informal sector at the expense of tax-paying, job-creating businesses.[20] Furthermore, the aid model can encourage governments to be outward-facing in their pursuit of revenue (building relationships with foreign governmental and philanthropic donors) rather than building an appropriate social contract with their own citizens, whereby taxes are paid in return for the delivery of public services.

Working in the informal sector is at best a stop-gap for many of the world's poor. Without legal recognition of their enterprise, they can face harassment from the authorities, have no official property rights, assets or credit history, and can be excluded from social protection systems. **To end poverty, we need to help these women and men**

transition from the informal into the formal economy. And one of the best ways to do this is through job-creating businesses: businesses that can help the poor to build asset-based capital, empower them through skills training (intellectual capital) and give them access to pensions and other social security systems.

Supporting small- and medium-sized enterprise is the next step up from microfinance. It offers the advantages of scale and size to create more jobs, improves tax generation and provides the environment for on-the-job training and learning, even if it is via osmosis. The merits of this approach deserve further analysis.

Enterprise priorities for tackling poverty

To address the 'missing middle' of SMEs, there are a number of helpful initiatives, some of which have already been mentioned (such as aid for trade). An environment that encourages SME development should also focus on: reducing bureaucracy to make it easier to register a business and import and export goods; simplify accounting and reporting requirements; and make available tax incentives. Reliable electricity, reasonably good governance, reform of the worst state-owned monopolies, transparency and political stability are also obvious prerequisites, and much progress has been made in these areas.

In addition, an ecosystem to facilitate SME development is needed. Incubator and accelerator hubs, government business grants, angel networks and venture capital providers are all components of this enabling environment. Because start-ups usually do not have strong revenues, they cannot be funded through bank loans; these, if available, have very high interest rates. As an extreme example, in 2009 the Democratic Republic of Congo's lending interest rate soared to 65%. However, a more typical example is

Kenya, whose relevant interest rate has been between 16% and 20%, or Botswana, whose rate has hovered between 11% and 17% for the past decade. Most businesses cannot afford to borrow at this rate. In most instances, patient equity capital is what is needed to feed growth, not short-term debt.

In fact, the lack of patient equity finance may be one of the single biggest obstacles to enterprise development in many countries, particularly in Africa. The angel and venture capital industry is nascent and under developed, and there are few viable alternatives.

One way to assist this sector would be through **loan guarantee schemes**, to encourage local banks to lend to SMEs, or through the creation of SME development banks. Could part of the international aid budget be allocated to creating and supporting local SME development banks, for example? A number of organisations are now moving into this space. Opportunity International now has a number of such SME banks in Africa. Business Partners and the Fusion Fund also provide credit facilities to SMEs in South Africa and Kenya. However, it is clear that the only solution likely to deliver results at scale is greater involvement from the business community and private sector.

A second priority is **access to energy**. In LICs this is often unpredictable, unreliable and expensive (with the exception of Ethiopia, which has the cheapest source of electricity in Africa). This reduces competitiveness and has a negative impact on growth and job creation. Businesses need power. Technologies for small-scale solar, waste to energy, hydro and wind are available and should be implemented. Promoting clean energy technologies can catalyse new businesses, creating jobs while providing power for new enterprises. Using small waste-to-energy power plants also has the additional benefit of clearing up the rubbish that blights many cities and slums.

Third, there is a need to introduce **more competition into key infrastructure industries** to reduce the cost of telecommunications, transportation and energy. LICs need to be competitive in a globalised world dominated by a number of the Asian economies. Many LICs have government-linked Western companies that monopolise key industry sectors. These monopolies are not conducive to encouraging new entrants into the market, which may make companies and countries less competitive. There are, however, some instances where government-linked companies take a longer view than private companies and keep costs low to stimulate the economy and give access to the poor. The Asian Tiger economies have done this successfully over several decades.

Why invest in sustainable, socially focused SMEs?

First, it makes sense. Investing in sustainable businesses creates employment in the developing world. Real employment gives people the dignity and self-determination to transform their own communities. This is in contrast to the dependency culture often engendered by aid. The strategy is to provide a 'hand-up not a hand-out' to alleviate poverty. Is it a surprise that poverty is linked to unemployment? What the poor want is not aid, but jobs – real jobs, not subsidised ones. One of the problems with aid is the need to keep asking donors for repeated support. In many cases, donor fatigue eventually sets in. With impact investment, funds can be provided either as equity investment or a loan. Donors become investors. Investors are more likely to take a greater interest in their investments than donors are in following up their gifts.

Second, encouraging the growth of SMEs has worked before. Thirty years ago, the South-East Asian countries were economic nobodies, economies based on low-priced commodities. Then Japanese companies started setting up manufacturing plants and were welcomed with open arms by Asian governments. Why? Because they provided jobs for their people as well as training them in new technologies. Within a few years, enterprising Asians, trained by the Japanese, began starting their own plants, often in competition with their 'masters.' The rest is history. Today the largest chip manufacturers are in Taiwan, Singapore and Malaysia – all locally owned. This is the Asian Tiger model. While the Japanese companies did not have a social transformational agenda when they invested in Asia, their investments nevertheless demonstrate powerfully how enterprise can alleviate poverty. The most dramatic examples in recent years have been China and India. This has occurred through the foreign direct investment (FDI) of companies from the United States, European Union and other Asian countries. If it has worked in Asia, it can also work in Africa. Africa cannot transform itself over any reasonable time frame without foreign investment.

Note to Chapter 3

20. http://www.un.org/esa/desa/papers/2009/wp89_2009.pdf

4 Defining social impact investment

The Rockefeller Foundation coined the term 'impact investing' in about 2007 but the core concept is much older. Over time, the term has been widely used and abused, so it's important to define here what we mean by it as an asset category.

Not every business that has an impact should be classified as an impact investment. The mobile phone, for example, has had a positive impact on the lives of billions of people. But investments in Nokia and Samsung products are not impact investments. Neither are clean tech and biotech products per se, despite Goldman Sachs' claims in a recent brochure that it is producing huge, global social impact through investment activities in infrastructure, energy and telecom.

Most big companies do not design or produce products primarily for poor and marginalised communities. So, for example, Tesla's solar energy cars and biotech companies' cancer drugs are for the rich, the middle class, and – if affordable – only then for the poor. The location of their operations also shows they are not primarily targeting the poor. By contrast, a mobile phone, medical or clean energy company intentionally located in the slums primarily to serve the poor would be a social impact investment.

Furthermore the impact has to be direct rather than indirect. An off-grid power plant that directly benefits a rural community would be a social impact investment. In contrast, a power plant with feed-in tariffs into the national grid has an indirect impact on the poor as it clearly benefits all the citizens – rich and poor.

Our definition clarifies what we consider an impact investment: **a for-profit business with measurable social outcomes that intentionally and primarily addresses the social needs of the poor and marginalised. It is investing for a financial and a social return primarily among the poor and marginalised. Any environmental impact is a secondary bonus.**

We apply five criteria to determine whether a business qualifies as an impact investment:

1. Profitable. Impact investments are commercially sustainable and profitable businesses. Depending on the investors, different levels of financial returns are acceptable. Some foundations require only that their capital is returned; others require a near-market rate of return. Some put social impact before financial return, others reverse those priorities. There is room for both.

2. Intentional. This is inherent in the definition above: these are businesses specifically designed and purposed to tackle poverty issues, such as human trafficking and lack of clean water, sanitation, primary education and healthcare. Tackling these social issues is their core business: impact is part of the means, not just a positive externality.

3. Local. These enterprises usually operate in the slums and rural areas where poor people live. This is their marketplace.

4. Direct. The enterprise has to have a direct social impact in their locality.

5. Accountable. Apart from standard financial reporting, these businesses report against simple and agreed social metrics.

Impact Investing is not corporate social responsibility (CSR). CSR is a charitable activity in which corporations engage to show they are good citizens and is a peripheral activity to the company's core business. There is growing cynicism about CSR, because all public companies now have a CSR report in their annual accounts; it is beginning to look more and more like 'C-PR.'

Impact investing is not socially responsible investing (SRI). SRI, or ethical investing, is a negative screening of industries deemed unethical, such as tobacco, arms or casinos. Impact investing is about positively doing good rather than 'doing no harm.' SRI would not meet the intentionality test on poverty alleviation.

Impact investing is not private equity with environment, social and governance (ESG). ESG are sustainability factors that can be layered on to investment analysis to identify companies with better long-term performance. They are not primarily designed to address the social needs of the poor. The recent B Corporation certification is a movement encouraging companies to be better corporate citizens with regards to ESG and sustainability.

Impact investing is also not green or renewable energy. Big wind farms, solar panels and electric cars are not impact investments. While these businesses may create employment, they primarily target environmental impact and largely benefit the rich and the middle classes. If Tesla were an impact company, Honda, Nissan and Ford could make the same claim. They too have 'green' cars. By contrast, off-grid solar power companies serving the rural poor would qualify as impact companies.

How do social enterprises fit into the impact investing universe?

Social enterprises (SEs) are enterprise-based solutions to tackling social problems. They are usually started with grant capital, and the social mission is more important than the financial returns. SEs tend to be small and not easily scalable. A few impact businesses start out as SEs but later take in private capital to fund growth to become commercially sustainable. Impact investments can scale up SEs so that they become profitable. We hope this happens more in the future.

The role of metrics

The social metrics reported by a business help determine whether it is an impact company. But there is no consensus here either. A number of organisations, including the Global Impact Investing Network (GIIN), have tried to standardise the reporting of social metrics so that investors can compare the efficacy of impact investments. But in general, impact companies as defined above do not have the internal capacity or skills to collect and analyse complex metrics. Neither do they have the funds to pay others to do so.

The Transformational Business Network (TBN) has its own unique set of social metrics. For example, members track the number of staff members living in 'standard housing' defined as brick housing with indoor flushed toilets and solar panels. This is because improved housing is correlated to improved health and is much easier to measure. Another surrogate indicator of health is to measure the number of families who have 3 meals a day. Regular meals, better nutrition would indicate better health. Members also measure who owns cars or motorbikes, and houses, to get an insight into changing fiscal disciplines without being intrusive. And, crucially, members track each business's tax contribution to the national economy. This is important because, while the right level of taxation and governments' wise use of tax revenues are valid issues, if revenues are insufficient, governments will need aid or bail-outs.

Others argue that we should move away from measuring outputs and look instead at outcomes – for example, that we should measure increases in educational standards to assess educational impact, instead of the number of pupils in school. These different measurement approaches further confuse people's understanding of impact.

5 Case studies of impact investment

This chapter contains examples from across the world of commercial for-profit social ventures that can also address the social issues currently being tackled through aid and philanthropic organisations. It also draws out some important lessons to be learned from their experiences in building businesses among disadvantaged and poor communities.

5.1 Education
5.1.1 Bridge International Academies (www.bridgeinternationalacademies.com) – addressing children's education in informal settlements of Kenya and Uganda

Bridge International Academies is an education franchise which Jay Kimmelmen and his wife, Shannon, started in the informal settlements of Nairobi, Kenya. The 'academy in a box' provides low-cost, effective schooling for primary and pre-primary children. The sizes of the school and class rooms are specified and lessons are scripted. The teachers use Nook Tablets for their lessons. Parents pay around US$5 per child per month via M-PESA, the mobile phone banking system. As teachers are better motivated and parents are taking a keener interest, standards are significantly better than in government-run schools.

The model required initial investment in developing an educational programme which can be rolled out across multiple locations. This allows for scale efficiencies, keeping costs low and providing consistent education for all pupils.

Bridge aims to educate 10 million children by 2025, as a means to help reduce poverty in developing countries. Educating the next generation is a path to development and freedom from poverty in the future. Bridge Academies is hoping the children they educate will help their families to escape poverty.

Their vision is to build 1,000 schools to educate a million school children in Kenya. The company is building an average of two schools every week and currently has more than 450 schools in Kenya and Uganda. Bridge currently employs 6,000 people and has about 1,000 teachers in training at any one time.

Bridge investors include Pearson plc, Omidyar Network, Learn Capital LLC, Bill Gates, Mark Zuckerberg and Springhill/Novastar Ventures.

Social impact:
• Bridge Academies recruits its teachers from the local population, and assists in locating and building schools in appropriate areas, providing employment and investment.
• With more consistent attendance from teachers and pupils, Bridge Academies is able to achieve better results. Teacher absenteeism at Bridge schools is around 2% compared with over 30% in government schools.[21]

Literacy results of Grade 1, 2 and 3 pupils are 50 to 100% better than those of their peers in government schools. In the recent Kenyan national examination, Bridge schools had an average pass rate of 64% compared with 45% in government schools. Pupils who have attended Bridge schools for the full 7 years had a 100% pass rate.
• Currently, Bridge Academies has 118,802 pupils enrolled in the 412 academies. Importantly, 49% of pupils are female: empowering women is a positive force for change, for current and future generations.

5.1.2 Silulo Ulutho Technologies (www.silulo.com) – addressing computer literacy and accessibility in South African townships

Silulo is a chain of computer training centres cum internet cafes in the townships of South Africa. They were founded by three former teachers led by Luvuyo Rani. Seeing the need for computer literacy among local youths, Silulo started in 2008 with one outlet in the large township of Khaylitsha, Cape Town. It offered a six-month paid course for a Microsoft accreditation, plus a business centre providing services to type CVs, business quotations, wedding services and other word processing documents on a fee-for-service basis.

Today it has grown into a chain of 39 township stores in both the Western Province and the Eastern Cape. In addition to its original services of computer literacy training and business services, more clients are also seeking assistance with their smart phones and setting up social media platforms. From an initial staff of just three, it now employs more than 150 people; several stores are owned by former students as a franchise.

5.1.3 Bulembu (www.bulembu.org) – addressing HIV, education in Swaziland

In Swaziland, the prevalence of HIV rose from 3.9% (1992) to 38% (2002) – a 900% growth, giving the country the dubious distinction of having the highest HIV prevalence in the world. With a population of 950,000, a life expectancy of 32 years and a population growth of –0.4%, the Swazi people could become extinct by 2050.

A group of businessmen led by Volker Wagner bought the 5,000-acre ex-mining town of Bulembu with the vision of housing some of the country's 120,000 AIDS orphans. They will be housed in some of the 1,500 houses at Bulembu and looked after by house parents in an effort to prevent institutionalising the children.

Bulembu operates on a social enterprise model. It owns a number of for-profit businesses, including renewable timber extraction, honey production and tourism. Profits from these enterprises support child care and education and Bulembu's clinic. These businesses also provide employment opportunities for the orphans as and when they are ready for work.

5.2   Eco-tourism and re-forestation
5.2.1   Kuzuko Lodge
(www.kuzuko.com; www.kuzukolodge.co.za) – addressing HIV, climate change, conservation in South Africa

Kuzuko is a 39,000-acre game reserve in one of the poorest areas of the Eastern Cape, South Africa. It has a five-star lodge offering eco-tourism and a safari experience operated by the Legacy Hotel Group. It is a 'Big Five' reserve in a malaria-free area and is incorporated into the Addo Elephant Park, the third-largest national park in South Africa. In addition to being one of the largest employers in a district with 70% unemployment, it employs a significant number of AIDS orphans, who are trained in a wide range of roles from game ranging to cookery and hospitality. The land has been rehabilitated, and in partnership with the South African National Parks, game has been re-introduced with conservation programmes for black rhinos, elephants and Cape Mountain zebra. There is a growing awareness among conservation agencies that, unless the economic needs of the poor are addressed, their conservation efforts will not succeed. A programme of re-forestation with the indigenous spekboom shrub is about to commence. Spekboom captures carbon and improves water retention of the soil and has been approved for carbon trading. With the carbon credit, Kuzuko plans to re-forest some 14,000 acres of degraded land over a two-year period, which will create 300 jobs.

The Kuzuko project combines conservation, job creation and social transformation. It is located in the Blue Crane Route Municipality where the main source of income is agriculture and the average income is half a dollar a day. HIV prevalence is 20%.

Kuzuko was recently reversed into a holding company, Inqo Investments Ltd, and became the first social impact company to be listed on the London ISDX stock exchange. The listing was to promote social impact as a new asset class to retail investors.[22]

Summary of social and environmental metrics since the project began:

• 39,000 acres of former farmland restored and re-wild as a game reserve in a region of endemic poverty in the poorest province in South Africa
• Largest contributor to the local economy, bringing in foreign exchange from tourists
• Jobs created (minimum one-year employment): 350, with increasing annual wages. Intentional employment of previously disadvantaged individuals (PDIs)
• Increased income tax paid year on year
• All staff in standard housing with indoor flush toilets, power, water and solar panels
• Conservation of three endangered species
• Breeding of disease-free buffalo
• Re-forestation of 500 acres of degraded land with spekboom

5.3   Rehabilitation

5.3.1   Agape Connecting People
(www.agape-cp.com)
– prisoner rehabilitation in Singapore

AGAPE's mission is to be Singapore's principal provider of rehabilitation, reintegration and resettlement services for prisoners, ex-offenders, delinquent youth and socially displaced people. The business is focused on two core segments: outsourced transportation and a call centre.

Agape was founded by Anil David and operates a 100-seat call centre in Changi men's prison in Singapore. Inmates who still have 12 to 24 months to serve are screened, trained and employed to operate the call centre. Rent is paid to the prison and inmates are paid a salary which is disbursed when they leave prison. Agape aims to re-build self-esteem and confidence by employing inmates and equipping them with skills so that, on their release, they can reintegrate into society and the marketplace, and thereby reduces reoffending.

Agape also operates a call centre outside the prison. Suitable ex-inmates are re-employed when they are released from Changi. The prison has initiated a programme of six-month early release for good behaviour, provided inmates work in Agape's call centre and are tagged. Agape also operates a corporate transportation business that employs ex-offenders.

5.3.2   Hagar International
(www.hagarinternational.org)
– supporting abused women and children
in Cambodia and Vietnam

Pierre Tami founded Hagar International more than 20 years ago to rescue women and children from trafficking and abuse. The stated mission of the Hagar project is 'to foster hope for vulnerable women and children in crisis through holistic, transformational development and creative initiatives.' Hagar was founded in response to the problems of street mothers and children in post-conflict Cambodia. It takes in women who have been abused and raped, rehabilitates them through a programme of counselling and then trains them to work in its growing number of businesses. To break the cycle of violence and poverty in Cambodia, Hagar believes in an integrated, three-pronged approach of rehabilitation, prevention and reintegration.

Today, Hagar has more than 600 children and women a year in its shelters. The Hagar Social Enterprise Group started three businesses that today employ over 300 people, mostly women. Employment helps these vulnerable women regain their independence, dignity and re-integration into society. A joint-venture with JOMA in Vietnam operating a chain of tourist-friendly cafes currently employs 200 people. Hagar's transitioning of its social enterprises to fully commercial businesses with a double bottom line return, has been both a painful and instructive learning experience. Hagar now has a sheltered home in Kabul, Afghanistan, and will be looking to start appropriate businesses for the women there too.

Rehabilitation: providing vulnerable women with the necessary life skills and income-earning capacity to transform their lives, by providing: a temporary home; counselling; literacy, numeracy, and health and nutrition training, and vocational skills training; schooling and day care.

Prevention: instituting interventions that avert women's descent into destitution, by providing training in literacy and numeracy, income-earning skills, children's and women's rights awareness and job placement. All education promotes community health (including HIV), empowerment, human rights, anti-trafficking and anti- domestic violence agendas. *Reintegration*: mothers and their children are re-established in mainstream society through livelihood opportunities in agriculture, self-employment, clothes-making or Hagar's micro-businesses.

Since 1994, Hagar has helped about 100,000 mothers, children and family members through its social programmes and economic projects. Although funded by charitable organisations and governments, it is seeking to be self-funding with profits from its commercialised ventures.

5.4   Sanitation

5.4.1   Sanergy (www.saner.gy)
– providing sanitation in the informal settlements in Nairobi, Kenya

Sanergy is a toilet franchise enterprise in the large informal settlements of Nairobi founded by Avi Vallabhaneni and David Auerbach. Toilets, built with concrete blocks, are franchised to micro-entrepreneurs who charge people to use them. The waste is collected daily, to be processed and converted into fertiliser. There are currently more than 600 toilets with over 24,000 daily users. The company employs more than 150 people and removes over 7 metric tonnes of waste daily for processing.

The social and environmental impacts are clear. Micro-entrepreneurs have a livelihood, people have better sanitation facilities to use, tonnes of waste are removed from the slums, improving the environment, waste is recycled as fertiliser and jobs are created.

5.4.2   AppSani (www.appsani.org)
– providing sanitation in Indonesia

Appsani is a toilet business in the slums around Surabaya, Indonesia, founded by Pak Koen. It is a different model to

Sanergy (above) in that it has a three-pit system that does not require waste to be extracted and removed. It also enables individual households to own their own toilets. Using a combination of anaerobic and aerobic bacteria, the waste is turned into water over time and is discharged into the water table. Teams of workers are employed to construct these three-pit latrine systems. Clients pay a monthly instalment to own their own system, which lasts an average of 15 years. To date, some 50,000 toilets have been built

5.5   Consumer products
5.5.1   PT Paloma Shopway
(www.palomashopway. com)
– catalogue-based marketing, Indonesia

Paloma is a leading mail order catalogue business in Indonesia, with more than 80% sales outside Java. The company was founded by Djunaidi Lie and is focused on empowering rural villagers, especially home-based women and single mothers, to become micro-entrepreneurs without needing any working capital or micro-loans. Indonesia has a growing problem with single mothers due to a high proportion of its population working abroad as migrant labourers. Men marry more wives and/or divorce their wives, often leaving them without financial support.

Paloma intentionally targets women and single mothers, trains them as sales agents and pays them a 25% commission on the catalogue price. Five new catalogues are printed a year to sell clothes, shoes, fashion items and household items manufactured by local Indonesian companies.

Paloma currently has more than 200,000 sales agents of whom 30,000 are single mothers. Paloma aims to increase the number of its stock keeping units (currently 2,000) and to double its active members within two years, with the goal of expanding into neighbouring Asian countries.

5.6   Food agri-business
5.6.1   Bee Sweet Honey (www.beesweetltd.com) – income-generation & environmental protection in Zambia

Bee Sweet Honey is an organic honey producer in northern Zambia, started by John Enright. It supplies bee hives to small farmers for them to manage. This outgrowers programme currently has 60,000 bee hives involving about 12,000 farmers. Honey is harvested twice a year when the farmers are paid. From this passive secondary income, farmers can earn two to four times their annual income from agriculture. The main use of this additional income among farmers was for their children's education. In 2015, the business produced 210 tonnes of certified organic honey for export to the USA and EU.

This business also has a positive environmental impact. Because of the income they receive from honey, farmers in the area have a greater appreciation of forest trees and are less likely to chop them down for firewood. The bee population has also increased as the number of hives has increased.

5.7   Renewable energy
5.7.1   The Paradigm Project (theparadigmproject.org) – addressing ill-health and de-forestation,

This project was started by Greg Spencer who designed a cooking stove which is 50% more fuel efficient and which removes 85% of the smoke and toxins that are so detrimental to the health of women using traditional open fires. Such fires are also a hazard, as well as having a serious environmental impact through de-forestation. This in turn has a knock-on effect on the security of women and girls: as they are usually the ones sent to collect firewood, they have to venture out further and further due to increasing de-forestation. The further they walk away from their villages, the higher the risk of rape. Girls also waste time that could be spent in school.

Paradigm manufactures its Jiko Poa stoves in Kenya and, through carbon offsetting, is able to subsidise the cost of these stoves and still make a financial return for their investors. By 2020, Paradigm aims to have impacted the lives of 3.5m people, saved $11.5m of household income through reduced fuel costs, saved 7.8m trees and traded 3.6m metric tonnes of CO_2.

5.8   Transportation
5.8.1   SPOT Taxis, Bangalore (www.spotcitytaxi.in) – driver-owned taxi services, India

SPOT Taxis is one of the largest taxi franchise in Bangalore, with more than 400 taxis, and operates 24/7. This was the first commercial radio taxi operator in India and was set up in 1999, with the specific aim of encouraging the unemployed to seek employment. SPOT stands for Self Employment Programme for Organised Transport. One unique feature of the company is that each driver is enabled to own his own vehicle with a structured loan over a three- to four-year period. They all have in-car radios and are directed by a control room using a computer system which tracks their location. This way, drivers make their money based on shorter pick-up routes and longer drop-off points.

SPOT has a corporate entity that structures the loans for the vehicles, equips them with radios to a uniformly high standard, operates the control room, trains and provides legal and ancillary support to the drivers. Through the corporate entity, it is able to negotiate vehicle leases with major banks such as ICICI on behalf of the drivers, most of whom have no credit history and would not otherwise have access to credit. Because of its buying power, SPOT has strategic alliances with Maruti Udyog Ltd for vehicles, Pulsar Inc for the electronic meters and Motorola for radios.

SPOT combines the management and financial strengths of a corporate entity with the entrepreneur vigour of self-employment. Unlike other operators, SPOT's fleet is driven by owners who operate as individual businesses linked by a common brand, system, processes and values. This, coupled with their reliability and high-quality service, differentiates them from other taxi operators.

Each driver takes on a Rs 60,000 loan. They make the monthly loan repayment as well as pay a management fee to the corporate entity for its centralised services. Average monthly earnings per vehicle are around Rs 25,500. Fuel and maintenance amount to Rs 10,000 and the loan repayment plus management fee is around Rs 8,000. Each owner-driver is therefore able to earn around Rs 7,000 per month. The attraction of owning a business within such a franchise has drawn people from all backgrounds and caste so that SPOT's drivers include ex- civil servants, security guards, police constables and the rural unemployed. It has been found that by running their own businesses, drivers are more motivated and therefore more productive. In fact, some enterprising drivers now own more than one vehicle. In addition to helping the poor to own their businesses and build a credit history, this is a model which is easy to replicate.

Lessons from impact investment cases
What do these projects have in common? Each was started as an impact investment business by an entrepreneur with the vision and the courage to take the risks. Funds were introduced into the businesses either as equity investments or as loans. The businesses operate in the mainstream and are run commercially. The employees understand that they

are not working for a charity. Their long-term employment is dependent on the success of the companies. Just as the Japanese FDI spawned new local entrepreneurs in Asia, so these projects expect to train and spawn the next generation of entrepreneurs in their countries.

The other noticeable feature of these businesses is that they can be scaled. Most businesses fail because they are under-capitalised and are too small. Social businesses that serve or sell to the poor on low margins can only be sustainable at scale. To achieve scale, these businesses need management as well as sufficient patient capital.

These projects help the poor with both employment and capital building – job creation and wealth creation. In our experience, helping the poor build capital, either intellectual (through education and skills training) or asset (ownership of a taxi, a cow or share equity), is critical to poverty alleviation. And the cities of developing countries are teeming with entrepreneurs who are creative, enthusiastic and resourceful. But like entrepreneurs everywhere they need access to capital and credit to start their businesses.

CK Prahalad estimated that the market at the 'bottom of the pyramid' (BoP), based on people living on less than $2 a day, is worth $13 trillion a year. While he encouraged multinational firms to address this market, we believe it will be more effectively tackled by local entrepreneurs through their SMEs. Impact investment builds businesses at the 'bottom of the pyramid' that have the ability to move up the pyramid into the mainstream.

But impact investment is a tough business. It requires business expertise and courage. It is riskier than a development project. Trying to get businesses going in the developed countries, with good access to capital and support infrastructures is difficult. There will be failures. But even in failures, people learn new skills and diehard entrepreneurs will try again and again until they succeed. In the USA, they call those who have failed in a couple of ventures 'experienced.' Starting and running businesses requires different kinds of skills to those present in the NGO community. Government funding for social enterprise should seek out the impact investment organisations, including the faith-based ones, to administer such funds for business ventures.

For impact investment projects to succeed, several factors need to be present. There needs to be trusted and experienced local management in place. As with normal businesses, partnerships with other companies and institutions to secure technical expertise and additional management support are important. Partnerships also limit the risks of the businesses. Many of these impact investment projects leverage local funding by acting as the lead investor syndicating other investors, soft loans and grants from government and development agencies. This kind of financial leveraging further reduces risks. Local funding often only happens as matched funding when there is a demonstrable FDI in place. Local funding also means local ownership which further improves the chances of success for the business. In most cases, these businesses empower the management and employees with some ownership of their business.

The single biggest requirement for FDI is investor confidence in the macro-economic policy and stability of the country. Transparency, good governance and an effective legal system are all necessities for attracting investments. However, it is in this very area of creating an environment that fosters business start-ups that developing countries are weakest.

In 2006 the World Bank suggested that future funding should be made 'conditional on cutting the time and cost of business start-up,' due to the money and time often wasted on bureaucratic processes. This proposal, using the research of Hernando de Soto, is designed to foster private enterprise. He contends, for example, that giving Africans secure title to their property would encourage private enterprise, which would by itself triple the annual income of the whole continent. Strides have been made in recent years to address the inefficient bureaucracy which encourages corruption and discourages entrepreneurship. There have been improvements: in 2015, the World Bank's Doing Business report highlighted: *'Sub-Saharan Africa, the region with the largest number of economies, accounted for the largest number of regulatory reforms in 2013/14, with 39 reducing the complexity and cost of regulatory processes and strengthening legal institutions.'*

The corresponding report in 2006 noted that it took 17 procedures and 165 days to start a business in the Democratic Republic of Congo (DRC); by contrast, the 2015 report showed it took seven procedures and 16 days. DRC is still 172nd in its rankings for ease of doing business. Sub-Saharan Africa in particular is still a difficult region; out of the 189 countries ranked by the World Bank according to their bureaucratic requirements, only six sub-Saharan countries ranked in the top 100; 39 of the bottom 89 are in the region, including the worst-ranked country, Eritrea.

Notes to Chapter 5

21. For more information, see The Wall Street Journal article (13/03/15): http://www.wsj.com/ar ticles/star tup-aims-to-provide-a-bridge-to-education-1426275737
22. For a press release on this listing, see: http://inqo.co.za/wp-content/uploads/2015/11/Inqo-Press-Release_ISDX-Listing-Final.pdf

6 Social impact funds

Impact investors are emerging from a number of different sources. Successful entrepreneurs and high net worth individuals interested in philanthropy have been among the first to provide capital for social investments. Some have crossed over from the micro-finance world to become pioneers of social impact investing. Members within the Transformational Business Network (TBN) have been doing social venture investing for more than 20 years.

Other sources of funds have come from the corporate social responsibility (CSR) area of public companies. One such example is The Shell Foundation, an independent UK-based charity set up in 2000 which applies a 'business or enterprise-based approach to deliver self-financing solutions with measurable social benefits that can be replicated to achieve large scale impact.'

At present it is involved in supporting start-ups and SME growth in Africa, reducing indoor air pollution and easing traffic congestion and pollution in large cities. Kurt Hoffman, the former director of The Shell Foundation, has explained his approach to business and enterprise-based solutions as follows: *'We think programmes are more likely to be sustainable if people are treated as customers – not victims. Through our work – and partners – we try to find ways to give people what they want at an affordable price. This requires creativity and an entrepreneurial spirit. In other words, we try and 'inject business-DNA' into all of our programmes. We expect our partners to think and act like businesses. If they struggle then we help them to do this. Admittedly, this approach challenges some of the traditional development community. During the 2005 Make Poverty History campaign we argued – in our highly acclaimed report Enterprise Solutions to Poverty – that jobs and economic growth should be at the heart of the war on poverty, not aid and debt relief.'*

Foundations are also beginning to engage in impact investment. The Omidyar Network was formed in 2004 by Pierre Omidyar (the founder of eBay) and his wife. The network has invested in a series of not-for-profit ventures, as well as for-profits, in line with the focus and values on which eBay was founded. These include inter alia a variety of micro-finance institutions, financial institutions in south-east Europe which invest in developing SMEs, a company producing solar electric light and a variety of web-based networks in a variety of fields.

Google.org, the philanthropic arm of Google that includes the work of The Google Foundation, also has a number of impact investments. One is a non-profit venture fund that invests in market-based solutions to global poverty, developing affordable goods and services to the 4 billion people who live on less than US $4 dollars a day. The J&J Citizenship Trust is taking philanthropic as well as loan capital from its healthcare business to make social impact investments.

The Rockefeller Foundation, although not engaging directly in social impact investing, has been supportive of developing the sector through funding research, conferences and initiatives.

In the last five years, we have seen a growing number of social venture capital funds as fund managers have crossed over from mainstream tech and biotech VC fund management to run social impact funds.

A table of some of the social impact funds and the regions and sectors where they invest is provided below (although this list is not exhaustive):

Name	Region	Structure	Sectors
Springhill Equity	EAC	SPV	Education, Sanitation
Inqo Investments	SSA	ISDX listed	General, SME
Novastar Ventures	EAC	LLC	BoP, general, VC
Garden Impact Investments	ASEAN	Pty Ltd	General, SME
Truestone Impact	West Africa	Ltd	General
Dolma Capital	Nepal	LLC	Infrastructure
Uberis Capital	Indo - China	LLC	General
Silverstreet	SSA	LLC	Agriculture
Fusion Capital	EAC	LLC	General
Africa Energy Access	SSA	LLC	Clean energy
Acumen Fund	India SSA	LLC	General
Omidyar Foundation	SSA	Not-for profit	General
LGT Foundation	SSA EU	Not-for profit	General
I&P Conseil	Franco Africa	LLC	General
SEAF	Global	Not-for profit	SME, General
Google Foundation		Not-for profit	General
Bridges Ventures	UK only	LLC	General
Africa Dev Foundation	Africa	Not-for profit	General

*   SSA – sub-Saharan Africa
** EAC – East Africa Community

Social impact investing

The early investors in these social impact funds include high net worth individuals, family offices and foundations. However, a number of financial institutions have also allocated some funding to impact fund managers: JPMorgan Social Finance, Triodos Bank and Axa Investment Managers, to mention but a few. Another recent significant development has been the participation of several European government agencies as investors. The UK government's DFID has allocated a first tranche of £80m from its budget to set up a social impact 'fund of funds,' managed by CDC. Norfund, FMO and other

European development agencies have also become investors in these funds. The European Investment Bank (EIB) has also recently launched a social impact 'fund of funds.'

These new investors are bringing much-needed capital into this sector.

A representative list of
impact 'fund of funds' investors:

Fund of funds	Domicile
DFID/CDC Social impact	UK
Norfund	Norway
FMO	Netherlands
European Investment Bank	Luxemburg
Triodos Bank	Netherlands
Axa Investment Managers	France
JPMorgan Social Finance	USA
Good Growth Fund	Netherlands
Good Society Capital	UK

A new asset class?

Along with many others, we believe that impact investment can and should be regarded as a new asset class of investments. (*From the margins to mainstream* (Sep 2013) World Economic Forum). This will be attractive to high net worth entrepreneurs and the venture philanthropists who have always wanted to see venture capital principles and accountability applied in their philanthropic giving. But it is equally attractive to institutions and foundations which have a Socially Responsible Investment (SRI) charter. Impact investment can be structured in limited partnerships in exactly the same way as classical venture capital firms. Perhaps to compensate for a sub-venture capital rate of return, governments can provide tax incentives to encourage investments in this new asset class. A small portion of money for aid can also be channelled into impact investment on a matched-funding basis providing those who wish to set up this form of investment access to government funds.

The role of venture capital in developing new industries, in sectors such as IT and biotechnology, is well recognised. In the early days of an emerging industry, venture capital funds are needed to invest in high-risk ventures with the possibility of high returns. Financing options from banks and other financial institutions are unsuitable for these early stage companies because of the nature of the risks. In much the same way, investing in SMEs in developing countries carries a higher risk than normal businesses. We therefore believe that impact investment is a more appropriate form of funding for these types of companies.

Finally, there is a need for listed impact companies to demonstrate that exits are possible for impact investments. They also need to appeal to retail ethical investors, moving them from a 'do no harm' to a 'do positive good' approach to their investments. For impact investing to become a recognised asset class, there needs to be an eco-system that mirrors the mainstream. There is therefore a need for more public listed impact companies, following Inqo Investments Ltd's lead (see Chapter 5), to establish this form of investment as a new asset class.

What more is needed?

At present, this market is relatively small, with about $50 billion of funds raised, and it suffers from considerable inefficiencies. Collaboration is difficult, there are barriers to information flows, there is a lack of businesses with track records of successful investing, and there is limited institutional infrastructure for the market. Also, many high net worth individuals and foundations still want to make a sharp distinction between for-profit and not-for-profit activities and so avoid this area. The vast proportion of this estimated $50 billion is represented by the micro-credit sector not social impact investment. Although small, some were predicting that impact investments would have reached $500 billion by 2014, which would have been roughly 1% of all managed assets. This was not achieved reflecting the slow growth of this asset category. One estimate even suggests it could grow to $1 trillion over the next ten years.

A key priority in this market is to create innovations that can achieve depth and breadth in a short time. Despite the questions which have recently been raised regarding micro-finance, it has now reached 200 million people but this took the best part of four decades to achieve. By contrast, mobile telephony has enjoyed spectacular success. The first commercial mobile cellular services were established in 1979. The World Bank, in 2012, said: *'The number of mobile subscriptions in use worldwide... has grown... to over 6 billion now, of which nearly 5 billion in developing countries.'*

We believe that three key elements need to be in place for

social impact funds to thrive and make a lasting difference on a large scale: innovation, incentives and networks of support.

1. Innovation – technical and business

In some areas, such as the provision of clean water in slums and the supply of credit in remote villages, local criminal gangs and cartels have prevented expansion. However, in other areas, there are real success stories, such as the affordable private education sector, low-cost environmentally friendly lighting and mobile payment systems. Innovation can improve the lives of hundreds of millions of people. To do likewise, investors will need to move beyond cherry-picking investments in individual companies to taking more risk with certain sectors.

Even if we believe that enterprise is the best way of tackling poverty, can enterprise also address the social issues of human trafficking, HIV, literacy, conservation, global warming and the environment? We believe it can, with some adjustments to the investment criteria. An experienced entrepreneur can look at a social need and design businesses that can address these needs while achieving a financial return. An enterprise approach to poverty alleviation is taken by building commercially sustainable SMEs that create jobs, empower the poor to improve their livelihoods and address their social and environmental issues. The same principles and accountability as for traditional venture capital are applied but adjusted for a triple bottom line return – financial, social and environmental. This is not an easy form of investment. It requires patient capital, local mentoring and capacity building. Nevertheless, we believe this asset class resonates with Harvard University's Michael Porter's 'shared value' investing and harks back to the holistic businesses of the Quaker era in what has become known as Quaker capitalism.

2. Incentives

The eco-system for this asset class needs to be created. Tax incentives from Western governments to encourage private individuals to invest in this way could be a catalyst for releasing more private funds into this asset class. Most governments allow tax deductions for donations to charities and transfers to philanthropic foundations and trusts. So why not apply the same tax incentives to impact investing that build social enterprises among the poor? Club investing, through a circle of friends or through crowd-sourcing, is growing and shows the appetite for this kind of social investing. There is a growing number of social venture capital funds mirroring mainstream VC and PE funds in terms of their structure and incentives. Again, tax incentives from Western governments for investors to invest in these social VC funds would be a welcome stimulus.

3. Networks of support

Businesses can only grow in environments that support entrepreneurial activities. It needs lawyers and accountants, and access to various types of capital. But above all it needs committed entrepreneurs and talented managers. Both kinds of human capital are, however, lacking in many low-income countries. Local talents need to be complemented by experienced advisors. In high-income countries, a company needing additional talent would hire the services of a consultancy firm. For a small business in a slum, such services are not available or not affordable. This is where outside networks can be invaluable. If a local business in the slum can tap into a network of experienced business people who can volunteer free advice on their business and marketing plans, financing options and technical assistance, these businesses will stand a better chance of success. These business people can provide the advice either as investors or just because they are motivated to do so.

A number of these networks exist. The Ashoka Network(www.ashoka.org) is one of the largest. Ashoka Fellows are highly talented and motivated individuals who have built successful social enterprises and are engaged in assisting local social entrepreneurs to build their businesses. Started by Bill Drayton, Ashoka Fellows and Ashoka-supported social entrepreneurs can now be found in more than 70 countries. Another example is the Transformational Business Network (www.tbnetwork.org).

TBN is a network of investors, entrepreneurs and business people who are disillusioned with writing philanthropic cheques and who invest their time, talent and money in building enterprises among the poor. Since 2003, the TBN network, which now has 1,500 members, has invested in more than 65 projects in 15 countries creating more than 20,000 jobs. TBN networks are being established in several countries to mobilise local business people to engage in this form of investment. TBN members are also creating various types of investment vehicle to attract more capital for social venture enterprises: revolving credit loan funds, fund of funds and listed holding companies. The Centre for Entrepreneurship and Executive Development (CEED) part of the SEAF Funds (www.seaf,com) has trained over 30,000 entrepreneurs in frontier markets. Meanwhile, the Global Impact Investing Network (GIIN) (www.thegiin.org) and ANDE (www. andeglobal.org) are forums that stimulate development of this sector in a growing number of countries. They are supported by the Rockefeller Foundation and the Aspen Network. TONIIC (www.toniic.com) is a network of social investors who share due diligence and co-investment opportunities with its members.

Such networks are challenging to build. They are often started by visionaries looking for innovative approaches to tackling poverty through enterprise. They tend to be funded by foundations or private individuals. Perhaps some international aid funding should be targeted at creating local entrepreneurial networks that are connected to global networks such as Ashoka, TONIIC, CEED and TBN. Such connections would help build local capacity, provide mentoring and, as is the experience of TBN members, lead to investment opportunities and long-term friendships.

7 The way forward

We believe that eliminating world poverty is a major priority for our time. Poverty, hunger, disease, lack of schooling, water and housing are a reproach to our generation. Increasing aid is of value and we welcome in particular the commitments which have been made on immunisation, vaccination and the provision of schooling for all. But aid will not create the jobs required to reduce poverty significantly. Aid is neither necessary nor sufficient to ensure sustainable development and poverty reduction in poor countries, but private enterprise is.

Encouraging enterprise is vital to achieving these goals. This fact is now well established and accepted, even by the large aid agencies. The dramatic increase in the provision of micro-finance demonstrates this, and it has been of huge value to many in extreme poverty. However, the vast majority of the micro-enterprises that this finance has created never become formal businesses or grow large enough to take on employees. This is a problem, given that what most poor people want is a job, not the risk of running their own enterprise. But the obvious solution to catalyse greater poverty reduction is increased investment in the small and medium-sized companies that can create these jobs, yielding both financial and social returns.

The way forward, therefore, consists of a number of steps. First, to encourage foundations, trusts, high net worth individuals and companies, through their social responsibility budgets, to invest in social venture capital projects, rather than simply making charitable donations.

Second, to encourage governments to devote a greater proportion of their aid budget to funding enterprise, and to design tax policies that promote social venture investments.

Third, to reduce trade barriers and invest aid money to empower poor countries to take advantage of new trade opportunities (by reducing institutional and infrastructural barriers).

There are no easy answers to the eradication of poverty. There is no 'one size fits all' solution. However, the role of enterprise – and particularly of investment in small and medium-sized enterprises – has been overlooked for too long. Enterprise-based strategies are the key to transforming poor nations and making poverty history.

Bibliography

1. Bauer P & Onslow C (1999) Fifty years of failure, Centre for Policy Studies
2. United Nations Development Programme (2003)
3. Dichter T (2005) Time to stop fooling ourselves about foreign aid, Cato Institute
4. Werlin H (2005) Corruption and foreign aid in Africa, Foreign Policy Research Institute
5. World Bank (2003) World Bank Development Indicators
6. Burnside C & Dollar D (2000), 'Aid, policies and growth,' American Economic Review
7. Easterly W, Levine R & Roodman D (2003) New data, new doubts: a comment on Burnside and Dollar's 'Aid, policies, and growth' (2000), Center for Global Development
8. World Bank (2005) Doing Business in 2006
9. de Soto H (2000) The mystery of capital, Basic Books
10. Prahalad CK (2004) The fortune at the bottom of the pyramid. eradicating poverty through profits, Wharton School Publishing
11. World Economic Forum (September 2013) From the margins to mainstream

About the authors

BRIAN GRIFFITHS is the Vice-Chairman of Goldman Sachs International and has been heavily involved in China in the past 12 years. Previously he taught at the London School of Economics, was Dean of the City University Business School, a director of the Bank of England and Mrs Thatcher's head of the Prime Minister's Policy Unit at 10 Downing Street. He was made a life peer as Lord Griffiths of Fforestfach in 1991.

KIM TAN is Chairman of SpringHill Management, a fund management company specialising in biotech and social venture capital investments. He is a partner and advisor to a number of impact funds including Inqo Investments, Springhill Equity Partners, Novastar Ventures and Garden Impact Investment. He is the co-founder of the Transformational Business Network and is on the advisory boards of the John Templeton Foundation, J&J Citizenship Trust, PovertyCure and Sustainia. He is a board member of the APEC Life Science Innovation Forum, University of Surrey and a Fellow of the Royal Society of Medicine.

About TBN

Transformational Business Network (TBN) is a network of business people and corporate organisations that uses an enterprise approach to tackle global poverty and bring social transformation. TBN supports commercially sustainable small- and medium-size enterprises (SMEs) in developing countries that create jobs, empower the poor and transform communities. TBN members do this by contributing time and skills, mentoring developing entrepreneurs, and direct investments in emerging businesses.

TBN was launched in March 2003 and currently has 1,500 members with 65 investments that have created 20,000 jobs. Our goal is to create one million jobs – and you can help us make a difference.

www.tbnetwork.org

Lightning Source UK Ltd.
Milton Keynes UK
UKOW05f2119020117
291132UK00012B/186/P